Thoughts & Beauties

poems by

Emily Dattilo

Clare Songbirds Publishing House Poetry Series
ISBN 978-1-947653-96-2
Thoughts & Beauties © 2021 Emily Dattilo

All Rights Reserved. Permission to reprint individual poems must be obtained from the author who owns the copyright.

Printed in the United States of America
REVISED EDITION

Clare Songbirds Publishing House Mission Statement:
Clare Songbirds Publishing House was established to provide a print forum for the creation of limited edition, fine art from poets and writers, both established and emerging. We strive to reignite and continue a tradition of quality, accessible literary arts to the national and international community of writers, and readers. Chapbook manuscripts are carefully chosen for their ability to propel the expansion of art and ideas in literary form. We provide an accessible way to promote the art of words in order to resonate with, and impact, readers not yet familiar with the siren song of poets and writers. Clare Songbirds Publishing House espouses a singular cultural development where poetry creates community and becomes commonplace in public places.

140 Cottage Street
Auburn, New York 13021
www.claresongbirdspub.com

Contents

broken mirrors	7
the part of you that stayed behind	8
say good-bye to hollywood	9
should've closed the door	10
sailboats and anchors somewhere on the east coast	11
tied together by the unseen	12
the gardener	13
antagonist	14
the truth isn't always a prerequisite	15
you aren't always right and neither are they	16
i clearly gave you too much credit	17
the wishing well is closed	18
before i had you	19
empty umbrellas full of rain	20
picture perfect	21
the ribbon we cannot untie	22
falling stars in the dusk	23
expired ticket	24
jaded are we	25
paint the sky with me, please	26
the question written in the sky	27
april 22 & april 24	28
same words, different meaning	29
purple shells	30
Please, Mr. President	32

The author wishes to thank *Miami Student Magazine* for previously publishing "broken mirrors," "tied together by the unseen" and "the ribbon we cannot untie" and *The New York Times* October 3, 2017 online edition for publishing "Please, Mr. President."

words form stories and stories form words

my mind is full of thoughts & beauties you
have yet to hear

twelve months told in verse

Emily Dattilo

broken mirrors

in front of her there lies
a paradoxical world of beauty and pain
the shattered looking glass

quietly accessorized with silent wishes
slipping desires and tainted experience

patience regained, she faces the world
reaching for things that cannot be touched

catching the open wind on her fingers
it's there for just a moment
only to disappear

because simplicities don't tend to stay.

the part of you that stayed behind

i feel
different

fell for him
reaching for this
beautiful.
my shirt smells of him

sits on the chair
I had forgotten

he
may not deserve me
but I cannot forget him.

say good-bye to hollywood

fairytales fade asunder in a sea of indecision.
turning the page. the past is evanescent.

close the chapter and cling to the rose.
the time has come to move from poetry to prose.

things are not what they used to be.
but you'll always carry with you the castle key.

should've closed the door

invited you here
where all i treasure most gather.
smiles and moments collected.
kills to know i gave you
the key.
watched with tears
in my eyes

as you turned
away and carelessly
threw away the key

that had taken
me everything to give

but cost you
nothing to lose.

sailboats and anchors somewhere on the east coast

disappointment wore smiles
thin
paper-thin scarcely see
what you promised
lays tattered though treasured
by one

it drops
shattered on the floor
pieces jagged tainted ruined
one leaves unconcerned
while the other stands there
surrounded by
broken pieces

feeling emotions,
though meant for two
that are dealt with
all alone

tied together by the unseen

you are not afraid to be
'nature's first green is gold'
light lilts
autumn leaves
thoughts and beauties
they have yet to see
crimson autumn beautiful
songs
and melodies
that have gone before
by artists who saw what we do

the gardener

i was June blue
purple violet sinking
slipping not believing

it takes the good ones
to pick the flower wilting

there are already memories
misting around your name

and now there are sunsets
vibrant orange yellow pink
memories to be made
clouds of spring green

all of which
i no longer have to watch alone

antagonist

i hate being the liar
it seeps into the unconscious
pricks my skin, taints me
the brokenness hasn't happened yet
but it will
then glass will fall, I'll pick it up

you're special
but this isn't working
foolish heart and foolish me
convinced myself
there was no way
it couldn't.

the truth isn't always a prerequisite

i fell for
the idea of love
enamored by
the petals i saw
in your hand
blissfully forgot
to raise my gaze
see the eyes
the person
the heart—holding them.

you aren't always right and neither are they

i stood tears streaming
clutching
at what was deemed something
i should cling to
they talk of love
but that wasn't it
it never was.

people said to leave you
my heart tortured me
in knots of indecisive
guilt and inexperience

the petals died
a long, long
time ago
folding inwards
i watched them, trying not to care

these experiences cannot be
bought
they have to be lived.

it wasn't love
but it wasn't nothing

i clearly gave you too much credit

and so we live
deeper than
most
taking solace in the bonds
that others
so carelessly brush
aside

taking, reaching
what i gave you- to hold
crushing, squeezing
breath out of
the living wishes in your
hands

one-sided hurt is so empty
you meant more to me
than you ever
knew

the wishing well is closed

non-sequiturs
colloquial conversation filling
the spaces with lavender ribbons
and little smiles
we miss.
close the heart and
put a time limit
on the wishes

because so often they just
are not coming true.
you don't need to pretend
anymore

i'll walk away
not because it's what i want
but because
it seems to be what
you do.

before i had you

i walked between raindrops
wrapped in uncertainty
weaved in unspoken thoughts
that i couldn't yet have

empty umbrellas full of rain

if it's here comes the sun
then why are we standing
in the rain ?

suddenly we're not
standing in a storybook storm
anymore

instead a single raindrop is falling
and in it reflects
the times of you and me

and though none of these
are in present tense
instead rather
brushed over

once wonderful
for someone someplace
dripping memories
encased in the bittersweet-ness
of what used to be.

picture perfect

you are the pure package deal
of heartbreak and disappointment
ribbon and bow

i allow myself to be
had by you
i let you let me fall-

those things, those pieces
i have to protect

have nothing to do
with you

but everything to do
with me

the ribbon we cannot untie

a new chapter unfolds
or are we not all
walking stories ?

returning to reread
to reimagine what went before

attempting to change
what we cannot
in our minds

words on torn pages
fading as memories do
flipping back
the picture is different

now composed of the good and inevitably
what we've tried to forget

old times
bound in sentimental ribbon
that we cannot anymore
untie

falling stars in the dusk

but now it's the fading echoes
of yesterday
composing what we kiss

and now what
we could have had
or might have had

is nothing
but a mist --

or maybe the mist
is dusted lilac
painted may
dreaming of peaceful
peace

and uninterrupted green
settled here
placed there by
one of so, so many

who doesn't quite understand
the way

expired ticket

and when anger
fireworks
from my lips

classify it misdirected
pain
wrapped in words
meant not for you

but instead
for some far-bound
mystery train

riding rails
scorching
unwelcome
magnificence

jaded are we

yellow flowers evaporated
in the breeze

and carefree carelessness
mocked the silence as they fell

haunting secrets
they never wished to tell
for flying petals to believe

only the best in what lies ahead
on the stagnated journey
to the wishing well

paint the sky with me, please

we have the privilege
of the
unknown -
colors swirl
and mix
on the palette of life,
so here's to
the painted sunsets and
sunrises.
the ones we
subconsciously
create,
simply by being.

the question written in the sky

and then i couldn't help
but wonder
did he like sunsets before us
or
was it just because
of me?

and when he talks about them
now
is that his way
of keeping me
when he knows
i am already

gone

april 22 & april 24

and so
with sincere—purposely
abbreviated
words by one
and
forceful syllables
crafted by the other
that's how
the two of us
said good-bye—

same words, different meaning

you said you wanted
your time back.

i want it back for you
because
maybe then
i could get a piece of it

too.

purple shells

    comb the salt of the   sea   and
    in   b e t w e e n
        broken coral shells

    perhaps you'll find
        unlikely streams of conversation
                we forgot to
                    finish—
    and moments
    we forgot
    to   keep—

    voices
        fade
          in   and   out
    thoughtless,
        mindless tease

    a poignant   night   shatters
        any thought
        of windblown ecstasy

    darkest   depths where
            songs
          don't
            sing

    second smiles strained
        caught somewhere
        between
            everything—

```
sand crunches
            underfoot
                        silencing missing shells,
tracing
            pathways
home...
                        trying to remember, in violet,
it isn't a
            happy place
                        always —for all.

sinking in
            greenery, riding waves
      still so much      to be
the world blinks in stars
      too far to count,
                        too few          to see

aging restlessly                against the blue
            oceans whisper
                        poetry and prose
brimming with hidden
      dreams    about which    nobody    here
                        cares to suppose.
```

Please Mr. President.

this is a plea. a hope. a wish
we rise each morning
Americans in every city
the newspapers scream
black headlines
thousands of letters smashed together
forming sentences of horror
deaths and injuries
numbers. numbers.
but these aren't numbers.
these are people.
people we cannot replace
people we never should have lost
people with families, friends, jobs
Please Mr. President.
we have so much ahead of us
our flag of red, white, and blue
our people embody this spirit
we are a land of wonderful opportunity
innovation, creativity, power
but how can this continue
we cannot be our best living in fear
fear that manifests itself in the unexpected
fear that turns to disbelief and regret
Please Mr. President.
these tragic events are far too frequent
something must be done
there's hesitancy now
a foreboding sense of caution
we don't know what is coming
i can remember
a different time
people didn't worry about movie theaters
malls. big cities. school. concerts.
that's different now.
but it doesn't have to be.
Please Mr. President
there are little kids growing up

protected for now by innocence
each proud to be American
but children are wise and wondering
they ask questions
parents fumble for an answer
they shouldn't have to taint young minds
with horrors such as these
Please Mr. President
this is a plea. a hope. a wish.
something must be done
these aren't numbers
these are people.

Emily Dattilo has written poetry since she was six years old. her writing has been published in Chicago newspapers and The New York Times. she loves painting watercolors, writing, listening to music and photography. "thoughts & beauties" is her first book.